Copyright © 2014 by Linda R. Barrett
All Rights Reserved
Printed in the USA

All rights reserved. No part of this publication may be reproduced or transmitted in any form or by any means without written permission of the author.

Cover design by Linda R. Barrett

At Random Publications
260 Lamar Ave #302
Pueblo, CO 81004
ISBN 978-0-615-98119-2

Table of Contents

Pocket Change, Promises, And Prayers

IV	Dedication
V	Author's Statement
VI	Promises and Prayers
VIII	Simple Prayer Steps
1.	Anger
3.	Blessings
5.	Confusion
7.	Death
9.	Discouragement
11.	Eternal Life
13.	Faith
15.	Family
17.	Forgiveness
19.	Gods Will
21.	Guilt
23.	Loneliness
25.	Love
27.	Marriage

29.	Peace
31.	Pleasing God
33.	Prayer
35.	Protection
37.	Rejection
39.	Sickness
41.	Single
43.	Temptation
45.	Trust
47.	Worry

This book is dedicated to two of my close friends. Carmela D'Ambrosio, you are lovely inside and out. I thank you for your kindness, devotion, and endless support.

Bill Long, I am blessed to be a friend with such a Godly man. You not only speak God's Words, you live by them. I owe you much more than a mere 'Thank You'.

What we do for ourselves dies with us…what we do for others remains and is immortal.

(Albert Pike)

AUTHOR'S STATEMENT

Have you ever been cotton mouth thirsty, searching for a pop machine to satisfy your thirst? Then you feverishly attempt to insert your dollar in the tiny slot, only to have it reject? Your fingers explore the deepest areas of your pockets and finally strike gold. Your challenge has been conquered in having the right amount of change to purchase your drink.

We all face dilemmas in life and require physical or spiritual change as well. God's promises will educate us in how to pray for the answers we are searching for. "Pocket Change, Promises, and Prayers" will help you with some areas you may be struggling with. Carry this book with you and refer to it as needed.

God's word provides insight to determine His complete will for your life. Read God's word as often as possible, memorize those Scriptures that speak to you, take time to meditate on God's word and most importantly trust and believe God's Word.

Prayer changes things, and your outlook of life around you will be clearer. You will also reap the reward of an intimate fellowship with Him. When you plead a heartfelt prayer, God is ready and willing to provide an answer; it may be yes, no, or wait. The Holy Spirit will connect with your spirit and an answer will arrive.

PROMISES AND PRAYERS

Prayer is no mystery. I've heard people say, "I don't know how to pray." Abolish that thought immediately from your mind, because if you can speak you can pray! Prayer is your heart-felt, most personal communication with our Heavenly Father. God does not expect us to speak eloquently. He just wants to hear us speaking to Him each and every day with the love we have in our heart, the plea for help, and the praises for his Holy Name.

Among the over 3,000 promises in the Bible, I am sure there is one you can find with your name on it, or with a situation you have encountered and don't know how to resolve. Pray back those promises to God, as there is power in His word. Take time to reflect on the days challenges and lay all your burdens at his feet. You are developing a close relationship with God and the connection is most intimate.

In (**Matthew 26:41**)NLT God said, "Keep alert and pray. Otherwise temptation will overpower you. For though the spirit is willing enough, the body is weak." Pray God's promises into existence. All of God's promises are yours! Spiritual blessings are there for the taking. We as humans are easily misdirected; however, God will provide focus through the Holy Spirit. So, have a humble heart, faith, be obedient and pray when the spirit moves you. I pray God richly pours His blessings in all conceivable ways for all who read this book.

SIMPLE PRAYER STEPS

Prayer is as modest as if you were speaking any other family member or friend in person or on the phone. Say hello, say what you want, give thanks for helping, listening and then say goodbye before you hang up. Psalms has the word Selah in many scriptures. This word is from the Hebrew language and means, "pause, and calmly think of that." Take time to think about what you want to pray and reflect on what you want to convey. Pray with sincerity, **(Psalm 145:18)NLT** states: "The Lord is close to all who call on him, yes, to all who call on him sincerely." Take some time to collect your thoughts or promises you will claim. Pray expecting an answer and be ready to do God's will. You must be prepared to do your part when the answer arrives, or you have prayed in vain. Answers may manifest themselves in a feeling of peace, a warm presence in your body, or a thought in your mind. If you are reading scriptures you will be led to find answers in the promises. I have experienced answers to prayer in a phone call or an unexpected visit from a friend. Throughout the Bible effective prayer includes fundamentals of adoration, confession, and commitment as well as requests; here are some suggestions on how to compile your prayer thoughts.

Address God: Lord, God, Heavenly Father, Abba Father, Father in Heaven. He is our creator and the one we owe all we have, he saved our lives. Praise His Holy Name in your greeting.

Thank Him: You can state specific things, blessings, or for listening and being there for you. I like to state: "Thank you for the many blessings you have bestowed upon me" or "Thank you for loving me when I feel unloved", you can state: I am grateful for … my family, church, health, etc.

Ask Him: Your specific need, clarification on scriptures, questions you have about your life. You can say: "I need", "I ask thee", or "please help me." "God is our refuge and strength, always ready to help in times of trouble." **(Psalm 46:1)NLT**

Close in His Name: In Jesus's name I pray, Amen. You pray to our Jesus who is our Savior, and Christ who suffered and died for us. Amen is said as it means we agree with what's been said.

The Lord's Prayer is also a powerful prayer that can be memorized and repeated on occasion. God will hear your heart as you pray these words as well. You can add your words of prayer with this, whatever you are comfortable with. Read the scriptures and hold close to your heart the ones that speak personally to you. There is no wrong or right way to pray, it is you having a conversation with your Father in heaven.

When I pray I feel it is not so much what I know, but what I say. Speak what is on your heart. **(Romans 8:26)**NLT And the Holy Spirit helps us in distress. For we don't even know what we should pray for, nor how we should pray. But the Holy Spirit prays for us with groanings that cannot be expressed in words. Our God is a loving and caring God and understands your heart.

Pocket Change, Promises, And Prayers

ANGER

Don't get angry. Don't be upset; it only leads to trouble. **(Psalm 37:8)NCV**

My dear brothers and sisters, always be willing to listen and slow to speak. Do not become angry easily, because anger will not help you live the right kind of life God wants. **(James 1: 19-20)NCV**

Patient people have great understanding, but people with quick tempers show their foolishness. **(Proverbs 14:29) NCV**

Lord, please aid me to control my emotions. I ask to have an open mind and a forgiving heart. My human nature causes me to get irritated and lash out at those around me. Please give me more compassion to see others are aching and that I should interact in a kind manner. Give me peace of mind and heart. Amen.

BLESSINGS

Blessed is the man who makes the Lord his trust, who does not turn to the proud, to those who go straight after a lie. **(Psalm 40:4)**ESV

Blessed are those whose lawless deeds are forgiven, and whose sins are covered. **(Romans 4:7)**ESV

Always give thanks to God the father for everything, in the name of our Lord Jesus Christ. **(Ephesians 5:20)**ESV

*My Precious Lord, I am blessed by all you
have created large and small. I recognize that
if I trust in you I will grow strong and never be
disillusioned. My many trials are lessons learned
and blessings in themselves. My faith will never
perish. I rejoice with unspeakable joy and glory.
Amen.*

CONFUSION

God is not a God of confusion but a God of peace.
(1 Corinthians 14:33)NCV

If you go the wrong way—to the right or to the left—you will hear a voice behind you saying, "This is the right way. You should go this way." **(Isaiah 30:21)NCV**

The Lord says, "I will make you wise and show you where to go. I will guide you and watch over you." **(Psalm 32:8)NCV**

Dear Lord, when I am in my most confusing moments I am confident I can call on you and you will hear my plea. You give me rest when I am weary, calm my spirit, and show me the way to proceed. Fill me with your peace during this time of stress and confusion. You lead me higher and for that I praise your Holy Name. Amen.

DEATH

We will all die someday. We're like water spilled on the ground; no one can gather it back. But God doesn't take away life. Instead, he plans ways that those who have been sent away will not have to stay away from him!
(2 Samuel 14:14)NCV

It is now shown to us by the coming of our Savior Christ Jesus. He destroyed death, and through the good news he showed us the way to have life that cannot be destroyed.
(2 Timothy 1:10)NCV

My sheep hear my voice, and I know them, and they follow me. I give them eternal life, and they will never perish, and no one will snatch them out of my hand.
(John 10:27-28)ESV

Abba-Father, the sting of death is tough to tolerate. Yet I know you will bring me through this agony. Help me to remember that death is a termination of life here in this world, however more significantly our final residence with you in Heaven. This spiritual death is a devastating thought. I pray for those who do not acknowledge you, that they will make a decision that will secure their eternal resting place with you. Amen.

DISCOURAGEMENT

Lord, even when I have trouble all around me, you will keep me alive. When my enemies are angry, you will reach down and save me by your power. **(Psalm 138:7)NCV**

Jesus said, "Don't let your hearts be troubled. Trust in God, and trust in me." **(John 14:1)NCV**

We have troubles all around us, but we are not defeated. We do not know what to do, but we do not give up on the hope of living. We are persecuted, but God does not leave us. We are hurt sometimes but we are not destroyed. **(2 Corinthians 4: 8-9)NCV**

Precious Lord, forgive me for my discouraging mood. I know you are the ONE who provides endurance and encouragement. I lift up your name immediately and feel you working in my life. Amen.

ETERNAL LIFE

This is what God has told us: God has given us eternal life, and this life is in his Son. Whoever has the Son has life, but whoever does not have the Son of God does not have life. **(1 John 5: 11-12)NCV**

The Lord watches over the lives of the innocent, and their reward will last forever. **(Psalm 37:18)NCV**

Here is the bread that comes down from Heaven. Anyone who eats this bread will never die. I am the living bread that came down from Heaven. Anyone who eats this bread will live forever. This bread is my flesh, which I will give up so the world may have life. **(John 6: 50-51)NCV**

Dear father, thank you for your precious unselfish love. The gift of my eternal life through your son Jesus is heartwarming. I receive your salvation and compassion. Amen.

FAITH

It is by faith we understand that the whole world was made by God's command so what we see was made by something that cannot be seen. **(Hebrews 11:3)**NCV

We live by what we believe, not by what we can see. **(2 Corinthians 5:7)**NCV

In all circumstances take up the shield of faith, with which you can extinguish all the flaming darts of the evil one. **(Ephesians 6:16)**ESV

O Lord my God of precious promises, my faith and hope are alive because of my salvation in You. I will call upon you and my imperishable shield of faith will be my weapon from all evil. Amen.

FAMILY

Do everything without complaining or arguing. Then you will be innocent and without any wrong. You will be God's children without fault. But you are living with crooked and mean people all around you, among whom you shine like stars in the dark world.
(Philippians 2: 14-15)NCV

Old people are proud of their grandchildren, and children are proud of their parents. A friend loves you all the time, and a brother helps in time of trouble. A foolish son makes his father sad and causes his mother great sorrow. **(Proverbs 17:6, 17, 25)NCV**

Father God, I am humbled to be a child in the family of God. In your goodness, You chose to make us your own. My Father watches out for my every need, and for this I praise His Holy name. Amen.

FORGIVENESS

I, I am the One who forgives all your sins, for my sake; I will not remember your sins. **(Isaiah 43:25)NCV**

When you are praying, if you are angry with someone forgive him so that your father in heaven will also forgive your sins. **(Mark 11:25)NCV**

Be kind to one another, tenderhearted, forgiving one another, as God in Christ forgave you.
(Ephesians 4:32)ESV

Dear Lord, I am washed from my feebleness, mistakes, and predicaments by your grace. I am a new creature to go and sin no more. I thank you for making my sins white as snow. Amen.

GODS WILL

First, I tell you to pray for all people, asking God for what they need and being thankful to him. This is good, and it pleases God our Savior, who wants all people to be saved and to know the truth.
(1 Timothy 2: 1, 3-4)NIV

Do not change yourselves to be like the people of this world, but be changed within by a new way of thinking. Then you will be able to decide what God wants for you; you will know what is good and pleasing to him and what is perfect. **(Romans 12:2)NCV**

Father God, Your will is what I desire in my life. Help me to find a discernible pathway toward a bottomless association with you. I pray for continued motivation and reassurance to come my way. You control my every thought and bring me peace beyond understanding. Amen.

GUILT

God did not send his Son into the world to judge the world guilty, but to save the world through him. People believe in God's Son are not judged guilty. Those who do not believe have already been judged guilty, because they have not believed in God's one and only Son. **(John 3: 17-18)NCV**

Let us come near to God with a sincere heart and a sure faith, because we have been made free from a guilty conscience, and our bodies have been washed with pure water. **(Hebrews 10:22)NCV**

Father God, help me to remember that I should not concentrate on the misgivings of my past. I have confessed all my sins to you. Thank you for your forgiveness. I will not forget your benefits to me I will not overlook your blessings to me. I thank you Lord for forgiving my wrongdoings. Amen.

LONELINESS

I will not leave you all alone like orphans; I will come back to you. **(John 14:18)NCV**

Be strong and brave. Don't be afraid of them and don't be frightened, because the Lord your God will go with you. He will not leave you or forget you. **(Deuteronomy 31:6)NCV**

"The mountains may disappear, and the hills may come to an end, but my love will never disappear; my promise of peace will not come to an end," says the Lord who shows mercy to you. **(Isaiah 54:10)NCV**

Dear Father, I was unloved and now I am treasured and have your promise that I will never be unloved or alone again. Lord, I want to stay close to you and seek you at all times. Amen.

LOVE

Those who know my commands and obey them are the ones who love me, and my Father will love those who love me. I will love them and will show myself to them. **(John 14:21)NCV**

Yes, I am sure that neither death, nor life, nor angels, nor ruling spirits, nothing now, nothing in the future, no powers, nothing above us, nothing below us, nor anything else in the whole world will ever be able to separate us from the love of God that is in Christ Jesus our Lord. **(Romans 8: 38-39)NCV**

Heavenly Father, as I attempt to spread your love on a daily basis, help me to love all those who are my enemies, and to bless them that curse me or hate me. Your word teaches me that love is a duty; help me to continually extend myself for the well-being of others. I must remember that as a Christian I must conduct myself as a goodwill ambassador. Loving each other is proof that we belong to you. Amen.

MARRIAGE

Marriage should be honored by everyone, and husband and wife should keep their marriage pure. God will judge as guilty those who take part in sexual sins.
(Hebrews 13:4)NCV

In the same say, you husbands should live with your wives in an understanding way, since they are weaker than you. But show them respect; because God gives them the same blessing he gives you—the grace that gives true life. Do this so nothing will stop your prayers.
(1 Peter 3:7)NCV

Father God, You chose us as your family as we choose a mate for love and companionship. You appointed we should go and bear fruit...The sacred union of marriage allows us to experience the greatest love...unconditional love as yours is. What a blessing to be secure in a loving relationship with the mate you have chosen for us to spend our life with. Amen.

PEACE

I leave you peace; my peace I give to you. I do not give it to you as the world does. So don't let your hearts be troubled or afraid. **(John 14:27)NCV**

The Lord gives strength to his people; the Lord blesses his people with peace. **(Psalm 29:11)NCV**

The God who brings peace will soon defeat Satan and give you power over him. The grace of our Lord Jesus will be with you. **(Romans 16:20)NCV**

Father God, I wish to be illuminated with your peace, please restore my balance. Create in me a clean heart, O God and renew a right spirit within me. I wish to declare words only of empathy, and extend forgiveness willingly. Shalom! Amen.

PLEASING GOD

It is not fancy hair, gold jewelry, or fine clothes that should make you beautiful. No, your beauty should come from within you—the beauty of a gentle and quiet spirit that will never be destroyed and is very precious to God. **(1 Peter 3:3-4)NCV**

So through Jesus let us always offer to God our sacrifice of praise, coming from Lips that speak his name. Do not forget to do good to others and share with them because such sacrifices please God. **(Hebrews 13: 15-16)NCV**

Precious Lord, I come with a humble heart. I do not always know what to say to honor your Holy name. Examine my heart and see the deep adoration and gratitude it contains. I will be faithful to you and am committed to honor you all the days of my life. Amen.

PRAYER

The Lord is near to all who call on Him, to all who call on him in truth. **(Psalm 145:18)**ESV

What am I to do? I will pray with my spirit, but I will pray with my mind also; I will sing praise with my spirit, but I will sing with my mind also.
(1 Corinthians 14:15)ESV

Pray without ceasing; give thanks in all circumstances; for this is the will of God in Christ Jesus for you.
(1 Thessalonians 5: 17-18)ESV

God in heaven, I thank you for always hearing my prayers. I come with a modest heart that receives your spirit and direction and grace without question. I feel your influence, splendor and affection always. Amen.

PROTECTION

But, Lord, you are my shield, my wonderful God who gives me courage. **(Psalm 3:3)NCV**

The Lord your God will go ahead of you and fight for you as he did in Egypt; you saw him do it. **(Deuteronomy 1:30)NCV**

He protects those who are loyal to him, but evil people will be silenced in darkness. Power is not the key to success. **(1 Samuel 2:9)NCV**

God, Thank you for your promise to never leave nor abandon me. You are my Rock and my fortress. Your strength is my strength. I praise you for removing my present struggles and providing harmony and wellbeing in my life. Amen.

REJECTION

God does not see the same way people see. People look at the outside of a person, but the Lord looks at the heart. **(1 Samuel 16:7)NCV**

Depend on the Lord; trust him, and he will take care of you. Then your goodness will shine like the sun and your fairness like the noon day sun. Wait and trust the Lord. Don't be upset when others get rich or when someone else's plans succeed. **(Psalm 37: 5-7)NCV**

Precious Lord, you are the God of all Grace. Help me to keep my focus on you and not the riches others may have. Restore unto me the joy of your salvation and uphold me with your free spirit. Lord I want to stay close to you and seek you at all times. Amen

SICKNESS

Christ carried our sins in his body on the cross so we would stop living for sin and start living for what is right. And you are healed because of his wounds.
(1 Peter 2:24)NCV

Lord, heal me, and I will truly be healed. Save me, and I will truly be saved. You are the one I praise.
(Jeremiah 17:4)NCV

My child, pay attention to my words; listen closely to what I say. Don't ever forget my words; keep them always in mind. They are the key to life for those who find them; they bring health to the whole body.
(Proverbs 4: 20-22)NCV

My Precious Heavenly Father, when any human healing is needed, I come to you first, as I believe in your healing touch. Secondly I ask for guidance for the doctors in making intelligent choices in my behalf. Thank you for always hearing my prayers for healing and wholeness. You are the light that brings me out of my darkness. Amen.

SINGLE

Now for those who are not married and for the widows I say this: it is good for them to stay unmarried as I am. But if they cannot control themselves, they should marry. It is better to marry than to burn with sexual desire. But in any case each one of you should continue to Live the Way, God has given you to live –the way you were when God called you.
(1 Corinthians 7: 8-9, 17)NCV

Enjoy serving the Lord, and he will give you what you want. **(Psalm 37:4)NCV**

God gives some the gift of marriage, and to others he gives the gift of singleness. **(1 Corinthians 7:7)NLT**

Heavenly Father, I am seeking your will for my life always, I realize my main purpose in life is to serve You and help others whether I am married, or single. The gifts you give, either marriage or singleness is your will for our lives and I accept your choice willingly. You know what is best for me and the path I am to follow, with or without a companion, I am at peace. Amen.

TEMPTATION

And now he can help those who were tempted, because he himself suffered and was tempted.
(Hebrews 2:18)NCV

My dear children, you belong to God and have defeated them; because God's Spirit, who is in you, is greater than the Devil who is in the world. **(1 John 4:4)NCV**

When people are tempted, they should not say, "God is tempting me." Evil cannot tempt God, and God himself does not tempt anyone. But people are tempted when their own evil desire leads them away and traps them.
(James 1: 13:14)NCV

Lord, I will hide your word in my heart that I may not sin against you. Help me to walk in the light Father, as you are in the light. Thank you for the blood of Jesus Christ which cleanses me from all sin. Amen.

TRUST

Trust the Lord with all your heart; do not depend on your own understanding. Seek His will in all you do, and he will direct your paths. **(Proverbs 3: 5-6)NLT**

Behold, God is my salvation; I will trust, and will not be afraid; for the Lord God is my strength and my song, and he has become my salvation. **(Isaiah 12:2)ESV**

Trust in Him at all times, O people; pour out your heart before Him; God is a refuge for us. Selah.
(Psalm 62:8)ESV

Oh Lord, have mercy on me. I have reservations concerning the world around me and I have encountered challenges I feel are difficult to conquer. Always remind me that you will permanently be by my side. Keep me close, have mercy on my soul, and surround me with your warm presence. Amen.

WORRY

Give all your worries to him because he cares about you. **(Peter 1:5-7)NCV**

My God will use his wonderful riches in Christ Jesus to give you everything you need. **(Philippians 4:19)NCV**

I go to bed and sleep in peace, because, Lord, only you keep me safe. **(Psalm 4:8) NCV**

Help me O Lord to defy the power of fear. I experience a sea of anxiety developing upon me. I plead for relief and the capability to reach the shoreline safely. Protect me from my anxious thoughts and help me to stay focused upon your word. Keep my faith strong. Amen.

REFERENCES

All references are taken from The Holy Bible.

ESV=English Standard Version
(ESV) The Holy Bible ©2001 Crossway
All Rights Reserved

NCV = New Creation Version
(NCV) The Holy Bible (Expanded) © 2011
Thomas Nelson Publishers
All Rights Reserved

NLT=New Living Translation
(NLT) The Holy Bible ©1996
Tyndale House Publishers, Inc
All Rights Reserved.

NOTES

NOTES

NOTES

NOTES

NOTES

NOTES

www.ingramcontent.com/pod-product-compliance
Lightning Source LLC
Chambersburg PA
CBHW060428050426
42449CB00009B/2193